ONLINE MARKETING SECRETS: WHAT THEY ARE NOT TELLING YOU

By: Mani Padisetti

To purchase additional copies of this book, please visit
http://www.online-marketing-secrets.info
This book is available for special discounts for bulk purchases for sales promotions or premiums. Special editions, including personalized covers, excerpts of existing books, and corporate imprints, can be created in large quantities for special needs. For more information, write to mani@onlinesalesleads.com.au

DEDICATED TO

To My Parents

CONTENTS

A WAKE UP CALL

Every marketer's goal is to make their product stand out from the competition – to differentiate it from the others. However, we use the same methods and tools that our competitors do. The result is that we are marketing just like them.

Additionally, often, we don't question if those methods and tools are effective.

It is true that the Internet has changed the way people make decisions. We, as marketers, use the same paradigms from traditional marketing as we move into the online marketing world. On top of that, we get "advised" by new consultants coming out of every nook and cranny that they know how to make our business work better.

Actually, I recommend that you outsource online marketing work. What is important is that you understand enough to "keep them honest".

This book demystifies many of the misconceptions and misinterpretations that are forced upon us over time. Using a metaphor – it's like taking the marketing we do from being on autopilot, using the programs and ideas that we learned at school or from other marketers, and stepping on the brake to help wake us up. By doing this, we can move forward, guide our own course and eventual success.

Even though this book is entitled *Online Marketing Secrets* – none of what's in this book is technically a secret. In fact, there are no secrets in business. There are only facts that you've not figured out yet. What we have here are perspectives on online marketing to help you break through the clutter. This book is not a story. It is a collection of about a dozen perspectives of online marketing and marketing, in general.

As Peter Drucker, a few brief words about who he is, said, "the best way to predict the future is to create it". There is an **opportunity** for every business to create its own future, if they know how.

My hope is that after reading this book, you will know the next steps you need to take in your journey to create the future you want for your business.

I wish you every success

Mani Padisetti

CHAPTER - ONE

DEVELOPING TRUST WITH YOUR VISITORS

When we are born, our natural instinct tells us not to trust much in this world. I t has been said that humans, over 100,000 years ago, used to hunt just with our families and nobody else. Why? We didn't trust them.

As food became scarcer, we needed to form hunting alliances and work with other groups. This was done in order to increase our chances of finding food, which led to sharing across alliances.

Even though our society evolved in that way, our nature still tells us not to trust people. Now, with modernization and industrialization, we are starting to trust people and give them the benefit of the doubt more often. In this day-and-age, we often do this before we decide a person is not trustworthy. However, our scepticism often comes into play here, too.

If that attitude existed in the traditional world, you can only imagine what happens in the invisible, online world - a place where we don't even know who others are?

It begs the question...how do we build trust with someone over the Internet?

The Importance of Trust

We not only need trust, but we need get more of it in order to be successful in our business. Trust happens over time and is a process.

Before we trust anyone, first we need to get to know them, then like them. Only then can we trust them. Trust does not exist when the first two elements – knowing and liking – are absent. When we trust the vendor, then, they can hope that this leads to us buying from them. It almost resembles a formula:

Like → Trust → Buy

Just the same way, we need to get the prospects to know us, like us and trust us before we can sell anything to them.

Making it Likeable

Marketing Sherpa is a respected marketing authority on the Internet. One of their guiding principles is that they don't like people to feel uncomfortable on their website. When the visitors are comfortable on the site they give themselves a chance to know, like and eventually trust the vendor – Marketing Sherpa. That is definitely a recipe for success.

To make it likeable, we have to make it familiar. For instance, we have to use colours that are often seen on other websites. URLs are usually in blue – use that. Don't use unique fonts. Try to do something that they've seen before. Make them feel comfortable. That's what will make them them feel secure and stay on your site to see what it's all about. Graphic designers try new methods and designs but if you keep the goal of making your visitors comfortable on the site, you will decide what is appropriate.

Even when pop-up advertising started coming out, with price offers or links to subscribe to free newsletters, people felt uncomfortable about them. So people often left websites that had multiple pop-ups and advertisers. Marketers had to look for other methods to catch people's attention.

Because of this safety factor, even Google, now in its own Adwords advertising campaigns, do not allow pop advertising campaigns. Now, what clever marketers do is implement delayed pop-ups. So the visitors feel safe on the website until the pop-up presents itself!

To double the trust, if we have a shopping cart, we can use secure servers and include a secure logo saying that the site is tested for safety. These symbols and testimonials add credibility to the site and also increase the comfort factor.

If relevant, show the awards and commendations your product or company received. Identify the associations you belong to. Then, people will know that you are a genuine business.

Building Trust

Now, once it is likeable through familiar fonts, layouts and images, you need to focus on taking it further and building trust with the visitor. Trust comes from the value that you are offering, not just the initial impression.

The value that you are offering is tremendous in order to feel that the company is one that they can rely and trust on. To build that trust, the most important thing we need to do is to think from the visitor's perspective and walk through the customer journey with them.

Question the way certain processes on your site are used by the visitor and try to understand it from their point of view. For instance, opt-in forms to sign up to receive a monthly newsletter or to join an email list, are great places to start. Think about how a prospective customer will feel when they see that. Ensure that you explain the benefit they will get from providing you with their information.

If you explain things and offer transparency, you will build trust with visitors. It shows you aren't afraid to tell them your intentions. This sounds basic, but it's a rarity in this day-and-age. As you build trust, you will see that visitors are more comfortable to provide you with information.

The Trusted Firm

In the book *The Trusted Firm,* Fiona Czerniawska talks about a four-stage process.

First, she states that the prospect needs to know that the firm has the skills and knowledge. If we are buying, we need to know that the product or service is going to deliver on its promise.

Second, we need to know that what we are buying is going to provide us with good value.

Third, they need to we expect to receive honesty, and, we need for them to tell us what we need to know.

Finally, a mutual respect needs to be achieved in that limitations are discussed openly. We recognize that everything and everyone has positive and negatives that need to be identified.

Czerniawska notes that once these are all achieved, we can begin to have *engagement* between both parties. But all the four areas need to come into play before this can be fully achieved.

Building trust with a visitor is essential for long-term success – investing the time today will allow you to reap the rewards tomorrow.

CHAPTER - TWO

IT'S NOT ABOUT YOUR WEBSITE

Why Your Site May Not Be Effective?

In a meeting of the Board of Directors for a company, Alpha Motors (UK) Ltd, there were two issues on the table:

1. Decision on closing down one part of the engineering department
2. Decision of the the colour and design of the uniforms for the supervisors

While the decision took two hours for the first one, it took 4.5 hours for the second point. Everyone had firm opinions about the color and the design. This ended up in arguments and a discussion for 4.5 hours.

Like those uniforms, your website is one of the most visible symbols of your organisation. Since it is also a "glamorous" job to be involved in website development, several departments or people in the organisation get involved in the project. Everyone wants their unique department and unique ideas to be represented on the website.

Typically,

- IT decides on the infrastructure – they want the latest technology
- Marketing decides on the site – if it is represented well
- Web designers want the site to stand out – it must go along with their unique design

- The HIPPO (Highest Paid Person's Opinion) walks in and wants to make sure that the site is worth putting their name behind – it has to make them proud

Guess who is missed in this? Yes, the visitor.

The visitor knows very little about your product or service and may not think like you do when it comes to searching on your site – remember, you are not the audience for your website; they are.

Which Websites Are Effective, Then?

Below is a site that may not be pretty, but it is 'successful' for its visitor-friendliness.

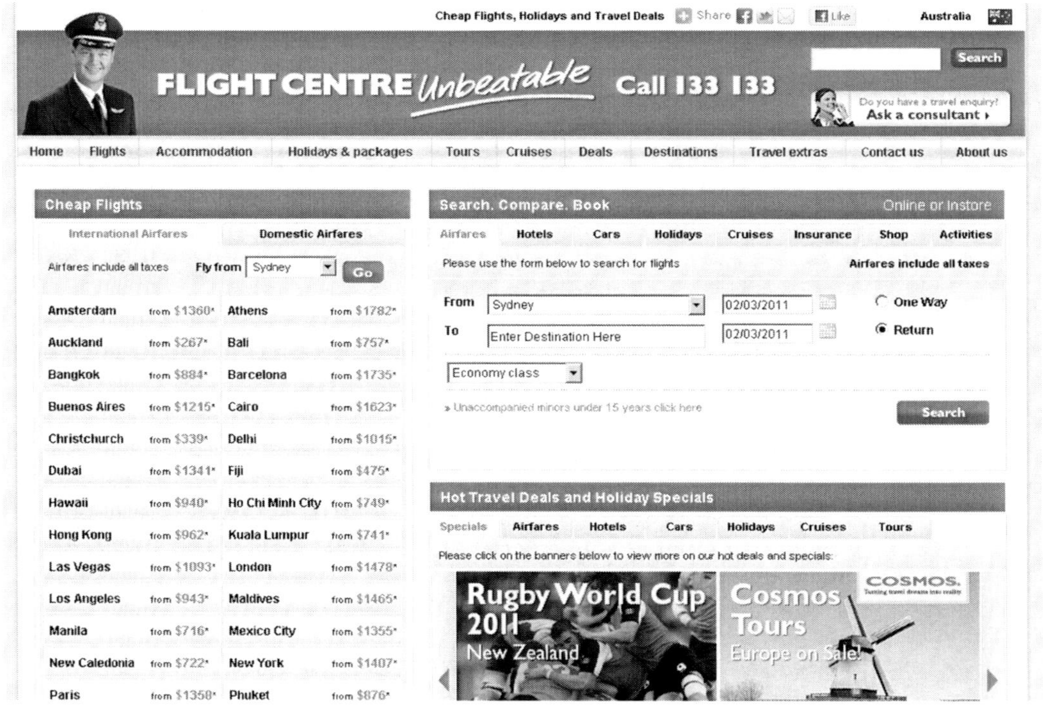

The URL is www.flightcentre.com.au. They've done their research, and they know people want a deal and travel options; not an attractive website. It is easy for visitors to get the information they need from this site.

If you want to experiment, try buying something from Amazon.com (the online bookstore). Even for someone who has never purchased anything online, it is simple to purchase from Amazon. Those who buy from Amazon, generally, buy from there more than from any other online book store. Why? It is simple and easy to use.

Most businesses don't know how difficult or easy it is for the visitors to visit and navigate on their sites – because they have not done usability testing or have asked for feedback from their visitors or customers.

OK, What Should You Think About When Designing the Website?

Some of the things you should consider while designing a website are:

- Visitors should be able to find what they are looking for quickly – remember, they are not you and do not need to know your website inside out.
- Telling your "story" is important and powerful but focus on the visitor or customer – what benefit, possibly immediately, does he/she get by knowing your story? For example, decide why it is important that your business was established in 1991?
- A clean, crisp, fresh looking website increases your site's credibility, but what is more important is its usability.
- When they land on your site, visitors decide in a couple seconds (or maybe even less) if they want to stay or not. Give as much relevant information as possible "above the fold" [i.e. without the visitor scrolling down]. In his book, Blink, Malcolm Gladwell, says that we all make decisions if we like most of the things we come across, in a blink of an eye.
- The Back button is the most used button on your browser. What does this mean to you? Think about it – if it is the most used button, it is also the button you want to avoid. This is why it is so important that your website loads quickly enough so that the visitor doesn't push the back button away from your site.
- In addition to loading quickly, it's important to make sure that the site loads without any errors and is easy to read. Design companies who create an artistic page can sometimes cause a lot of issues in this area as the design may be nice but the text isn't easy on the eye. For example, white text on a black background might look nice but it is hard to read. Arial or Verdana font and a size of 11 or 12 are ideal. This may not give you a website of beauty, but it's better to have a website people can read than one that is beautiful.

- The standard web design is:

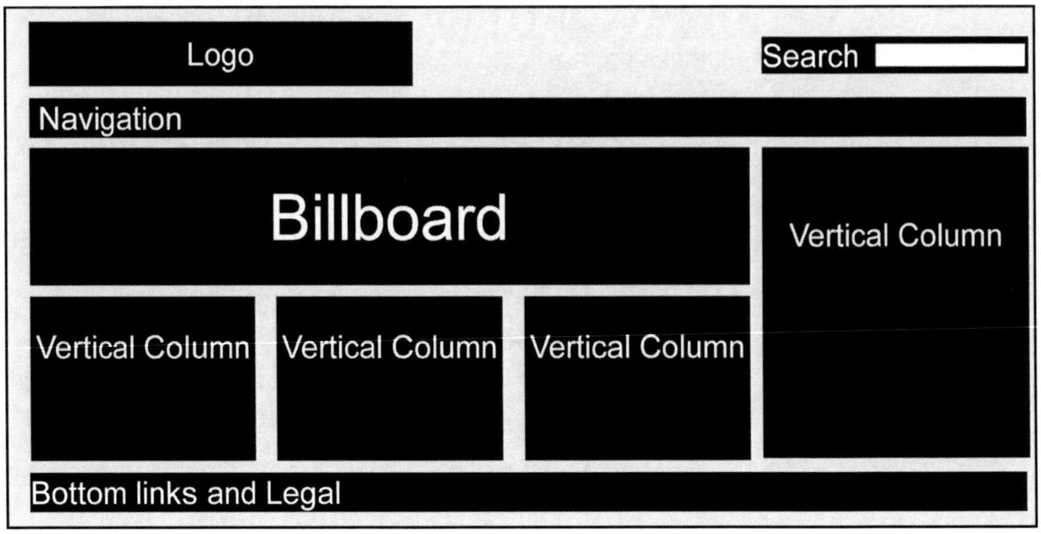

The issue with the above standard design is that most of the valuable space is taken away by "billboard" – be it a header or a flash element. You could use that space for conveying an important message. Maybe you can flip that design and have the following:

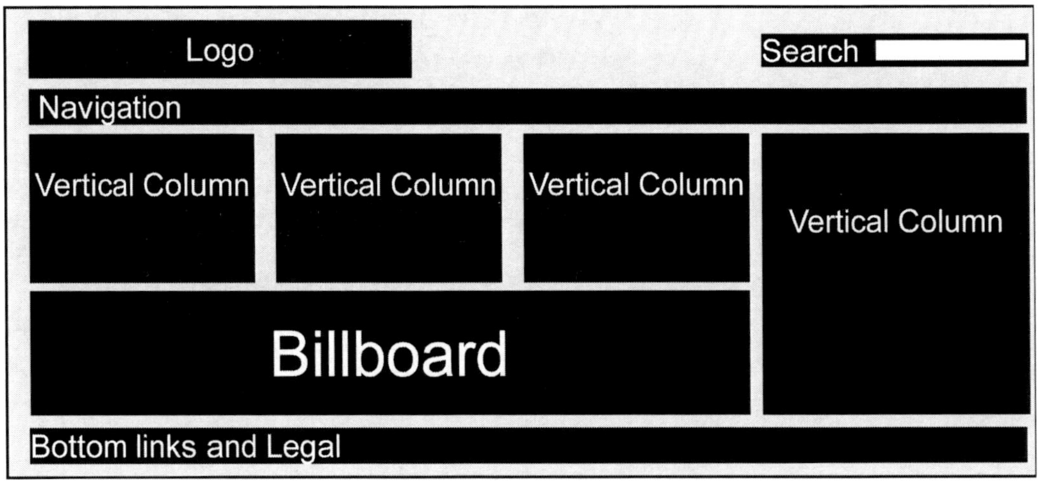

Test and find out which one works better for you.

One last point I want to make is this: please don't let a designer, "marketer " or an IT professional make the design decisions.

"But my manager says our website must maintain our branding"

Marketers tend to think of branding as a "sensitive," "softer" concept. Perhaps that is why the websites they make are easy on the eye with some appealing pictures. Jeff Bezos, of Amazon.com said once, "Branding is what they say about you (or your product), when you leave the room". Branding is just the reputation. The reputation is earned. It doesn't come as the result of an appealing website. It comes by making the site easy for the visitors to communicate, contact, and do business with you.

If marketing is about understanding what the user wants and giving them it, then the goal is to understand the users' wants and give it to them.

If you are already using your website to generate income, whether with a shopping cart, for sales leads, for investor relations, or for PR, find a way to observe your visitors. Then, help the visitors to use the site well.

Simple Usability Testing

When a visitor comes to our website, they come to complete a task – looking for information about our product, looking to get your address, looking to see if you have any job vacancies, etc. Identify what tasks your visitors are there for, and then get someone from your target audience to complete the task. Get feedback on how easy or difficult it was to complete the task. This is the best and efficient way of completing a "usability test" for your website. As a first step, do this for your site, today!

If your current website is organised based on your organisational structure or on the departments you have, your usability test should tell you that you that the site should be organised by the type of tasks people do on the site and not on the departments!

Specialized Service Providers

If you are developing a completely new website, what follows is very important. Often companies want to use a website development company that creates websites specific to their industry.

As a marketer, if I do work for one particular industry in marketing, these skills easily translate to other industries. The same goes for IT professionals and even accountants.

Using IT as an example, 80% of IT problems are typically common across the industries and 20% are unique to that specific industry. The 20% uniqueness is due to unique systems, software, terminology or customers. By going to an industry-specific supplier, you may actually be doing yourself a disservice.

The industry – specific supplier may charge more for their insight into the industry that you are already aware of but lack expertise in the area you need them the most – designing the website. Be aware.

Website Renovation

Far too often, I see businesses doing a makeover to their website because, they say, it is stale. They rearrange the sections and change the images to give a fresh look. The truth is that the customers and visitors don't care about the look of the website.

There are billions of web pages – a lot of them have "filler" (or useless) information and some have excellent quality information; a lot of web pages have attractive pictures and flash rolling all over. We all have been on the Internet for several years now, and the novelty of the flashy stuff has worn off.

We go to the Internet because it empowers us and, without the annoying ads or sales people, we get the information we want. We are seriously looking for relevant and insightful information.

So, you don't need to refurbish the looks of your website. Work on giving the highest quality education and information to your visitors. People don't leave if you don't have a beautiful website. Actually, they don't think about it at all. I've spent hours on the Microsoft site looking for specific information – I didn't care about the site aesthetics or how long it was taking to find that information. Since the information was important to me, I stayed on the website. Plan on giving great content to your visitors and stop wasting your time and money on renovating the site.

What Should You Do Now?

To start on the path of developing your site, here are a few things you can do:

- Explore what the goals of your website are. Make sure you are convinced of the goals. Typically, websites have the following goals:
  - Generate leads or acquire customers
  - Sell more to existing customers
  - Create branding and/or awareness

- Reach the journalists
- Investor relations
- Help existing customers' problems (through support)
- Sell goods and services to new customers
- Put yourself in your visitors' shoes and explore how your website is being used by the visitors. Write down what improvements you need to make, discuss with your team, and implement.
- Test the changes. Measure the results.

A good book to read on this subject is "Don't make me think" by Steve Krug.

CHAPTER - THREE

GRADUATING THE PRINCE INTO A KING

Websites and online marketing have evolved.

At first, we were fascinated with how websites looked, and what they did. As a society, we have moved past the days of being wowed by Ajax or Flash animations on the websites. The novelty has worn off, and we now all realize what is most important – the content.

Is Content Actually King?

We have a saying in the online marketing world, "Content is King".

Actually, if you look at websites today, the content there isn't close to being a king – not even a prince. Much of what we see today, unfortunately, is "filler content".

As marketers we want to get better rankings in the search engines. We already know that search engines will give better rankings to the sites that have regular fresh content, among other factors. So, we get some content together, sprinkle in the keywords so the search engines will notice us, and publish. That is what most marketers that keep their website regularly updated do!

The fear they have is that if you don't have content, people won't visit your site. The truth is they will come to your site if you get better rankings but if the content is not interesting and relevant, they will leave.

Relevance to the Reader

We live in a world where it is easy to create content – it surrounds us every day and is almost everywhere we go. What we really need to do to make content King is to make the information relevant for users so it is interesting to them. This point needs to be reinforced over and over again – relevance is what makes content King.

An Example

Let us take an example of a website for a pharmaceutical company. The researchers were producing content for the drugs they manufactured. The regular content included information on chemicals, on drugs, on side effects, and its uses. They focussed on educating the medical practitioners – primarily the doctors.

To determine who was accessing the content the most, they conducted a survey. They found out that the people who found the content most useful wasn't doctors but were the care givers. In most families, this is the mothers.

The pharmaceutical company had to change the way they were writing – mothers don't need a technical approach, but a practical one.

The researchers in the pharmaceutical company found a casual style of writing a bit uncomfortable as they weren't used to writing for mothers. In order to make the content relevant and interesting, though, the writing had to change. The readership had now changed so the content needed to change as well. This example demonstrates the importance of relevance of the information. Even if we, as the site owners, don't like the content style, we write it for the reader.

The Bottom Line.

Creating engaging content is easy. First we need to know who our readers are. Then, we must ask ourselves, when we are writing, if the content addresses the needs of the reader.

Many online marketers create a persona so that it is easier to focus on that target audience. By doing this, as in the example above, you can visualize a person who you are writing to. The interests of the mother then can be questioned and relevance taken into account.

Creating this type of content will help in the search engines and also help to convert the readers into customers. If we disregard our readers, conversion is likely not to happen. People will feel uncomfortable and leave the website. By writing relevant content, we build trust, and we grow our customer base.

By taking these steps and committing to create quality and relevant content, we can truly make content King and convert leads into hard sales for the business.

CHAPTER - FOUR

STOP WASTING YOUR MARKETING DOLLARS

There are many places you can spend your marketing dollars – from websites that you can place a banner ad, to print publications, to advertising spots on the radio or TV.

The first question you need to ask is what results you expect. You're likely to get an answer about their circulation numbers or audience numbers or the number of visits to their site in a day.

On the surface, these are hard numbers, but they are not telling you exactly what numbers your campaign will generate, for you.

Take a Stand

I suggest that you stop spending money on marketing or advertising activities that you cannot measure and monitor. Put this in place as a policy: nobody spends money on ads or marketing, if they can't measure the results.

Once you can measure the results, then you can see if a campaign is successful.

Be Realistic

It may not be possible sometimes to gain direct customers from a campaign, but you can and should expect for the number of visits to increase and to generate leads. Be clear with those involved in the campaign on your expectations and assign accountability to those individuals for the success of a campaign.

So what's all this talk about Facebook or Tweeting?

Many times, marketing is blamed for just "selling the sizzle" without giving a steak! The "hype factor" is abundant in marketing. I am not entirely sure why but, there is more hype than usual when it comes to Internet marketing.

Every other day there is someone claiming that they have achieved #1 position in Google (for a very competitive keyword) and have stayed in that position for several months. There are some others that claim that they have made millions on the Internet. Yet, few others say they have "cheated" Google in its own game, and they are ready to teach us!

If they really did "cheat" Google, then it won't be too long before Google "sandboxes" them.

No wonder people who genuinely want to use Internet marketing services get sceptical.

Hype is empty and baseless promises, or falsified claims.

In that spirit, let me explain a couple phenomenons (especially, if you had thought Internet advertising, SEO, or social marketing will solve all the current problems in your organization).

1. Yes, you can generate leads online. Did you know that many organizations get leads and do nothing with them or still go broke? So, the leads are not going to solve any problem until you follow up with them, close the sale, and collect the money.

I know of an organization that thought it could solve many issues in the Sales Department by implementing a Customer Relationship Management (CRM) system. However, even after it "went live," the sales people continued to maintain their own spreadsheets for commission calculations. They didn't input the details of the leads or update the progress of the leads until they closed the sales. The boss later realized that the sales staff didn't want to give away the information about the leads, because the sales force considered it was "their power". CRM is just an enabler, like Internet marketing is.

You need to have your processes in order to convert the leads into long-term customers; you need to spend time (whether you outsource or do this work in-house) testing and improving various elements in your marketing. Then, invest your money to make the process work.

2. You may come across people talking about "viral marketing" or how their Twitter, Facebook, or Blog is doing wonders for their business.

Maybe you get motivated enough to start a Blog or Facebook page. You see no results and give up, thinking that it doesn't work. Most of the time, the execution is the key and sometimes, it may not be the right thing for your business or situation. Maybe, email marketing will be more suitable for you instead of a Twitter campaign.

Don't start doing what others are doing because it may have worked for them or someone suggested it. There is no problem in trying something new but analyse the process and understand it before you dip your toes.

The data you get from your analytics software can never be 100% accurate or precise (nothing is!), but you will be able to make good judgments and decisions if you interpret it correctly. Learn how to read them. Analyse and understand what the market is telling you before you do an email or Twitter campaign.

Don't waste money getting into Internet advertising to appear cool or hip! Test it and take small, calculated risks.

CHAPTER - FIVE

INEXPENSIVE WAY TO DEVELOP A BOND

In my business, I work with many clients who are in different states of Australia and around the world. As we work across regions with a number of people, we start to realize how well we can get to know someone even without seeing them, face-to-face or, in some instances, never speaking to them. Over time we build an understanding with one another and feel close. All of us feel that even though we only speak through email, we have a strong relationship and a strong understanding of one another's needs.

Underestimating the Power of Email

Even though we do this day in and day out for both personal and work-related reasons, many of us underestimate the power of the email channel. When you take a step back and look at it, email is one of the most personal mediums we have today that are used by a marketer.

It is private conversations between two people. It is one of the surreptitious ways to communicate with your prospects and customers – competitors don't know what you are doing. Email marketing is the most cost-effective way to communicate and work with the least mark on the environment.

Segmenting for Success

With email, we can segment our database and create different distribution lists or email groups. This can include a list of existing customers who use a particular product, customers who fit the profile for another product set to come out on the market, prospective customers who have never bought anything from you, or individuals in a particular region of the world we want to inform. We can also use psychographic profiles to segment our database and send specific messages to these groups.

Email Abuse and Misuse

Often, as marketers, we either abuse or misuse the email channel.

Marketers abuse emails often by sending messages that are not specific or relevant – for the sole mistake of the prospects giving their emails! There is a view in the community that we need to message customers frequently. Yes, it is important to keep the frequency and momentum, but what are we saying to them may be ineffective or even, SPAM.

However, if we develop email content that is informative and helps a customer, we can make our mark. We can send out case studies highlighting issues that other customers had, information on what we did to resolve them, provide tips on things they may not know about the product or service, and helpful hints on how to select a provider for a particular service. Educational emails are very powerful as they are interesting and not a sales push. Customers will buy when they do not feel forced to buy. Create a bond by helping them, and they will reciprocate by buying from you, when they are ready.

Email newsletters are great but if they are generic and have no relevance to a customer, they will not help your marketing. For very sentence you write in your email, always ask "So what?" so you can remember why a customer would want to read your email.

Once, I came across a marketer who was selling copywriting services. He sent an email every day to his customers, with fresh and useful content. The result? – They were widely read, recipients were happy, and it helped grow his business. He wanted to prove that a.) We can write useful content for the reader, if we are committed and b). Helpful content increases the relationship and, therefore, sales.

You're Not Going to Satisfy Everyone

There are always going to be people who don't want to receive emails every day, and they will unsubscribe. Write personal emails – let your personality come through in what you write. By demonstrating your personality in your emails, you at least let them know who you are. If they don't like your personality, then they will unsubscribe. It's better to let them know you as soon as you can to determine if they appreciate you. They will then join you, rather than find out that you are not a perfect match, after investing a lot of time and money.

It's important to use email as your way of communicating personally with customers. If it's generic and cold, why would they want to read it? They could read that on an ad or a billboard. Even when you are writing for a group, imagine you are writing for one person. That's the secret of writing personalised messages.

Getting Customers to Read Emails

Some people say the most important thing in email marketing is that it's delivered. I won't dispute that - it is important for your email to go into the inbox versus junk or SPAM mail.

Secondly, many say, it is ensuring that your email is opened. Clever ways can be developed to entice customers using interesting subject lines. There are even courses nowadays to show marketers how to make the subject line tempting. Personally, I don't think this is useful and it may even work against you versus benefiting you. However, once they open it, and the content doesn't match the subject, you've lost trust and credibility. The next time you send an email it won't be read, and you'll be filed in the junk bin.

The Power of Reputation

What's more important than a clever subject line is building a solid and trusted reputation as an individual and a company. We all receive emails from firms and people daily, and most of us can weed out the good and the bad pretty quickly. I know that there are emails I receive, that as soon as I see the sender, I know it will have quality content – so I open it. The respect is built on the reputation for delivering interesting information to me – their customer.

What to Know

As marketers we know emails are a form of communication that is here to stay.

Remember these quick points for email success:

- **Not all emails can read html well** – either write two types of email (html or plain text) OR include a plain text link in the email that redirects the visitor to your website;
- **Be creative** – embed videos, relevant links to your website, and free PDF downloads in the email;
- **There is no right or wrong when it comes to email length** – make it as long as it needs to be – shorter is better, but not at the risk of losing the value. If you want to keep it short, add links and videos so that you ensure you communicate what you need to.

CHAPTER - SIX

KEYWORD MAGIC

Keywords are the terms that an individual uses to reach your site. The concept of keyword is more powerful than the mighty Google. With its secrets and mystical overtones, the ideas have become more confusing than necessary.

Since most purchasing decisions start out with an online search, it is more important than ever to have a high ranking in the Search Engines for the keywords your prospects use to locate the type of product or service that you offer.

From reading this chapter, you should be able to understand keywords.

Keyword Tools

There are companies that actually use tools and specialise in keyword research. As these businesses are doing well, there is obviously a need in the marketplace to get search ranking right first.

Google has a tool to analyse keyword effectiveness. It is called the Google Adwords Search (http://www.google.com/sktool/#). This tool is enough to do keyword research. You don't need a specialist.

Broad to Narrow

As an individual, think about how you search. For example, if you are looking for a used car, the first thing you'd likely enter in a search engine is "used car". As you progress with the research, you typically drill it further down to include brand, colour, model, price range, kilometres, warranty and a number of other factors that are of interest to you. This process would continue until you come up with a specific keyword phrase like "Toyota Camry 2009 with no more than 50,000 kilometres". From this example, you see that something that started from a broad search, ended with something very specific.

The narrow keyword is called the buy keyword. This is, essentially, the keyword that will drive" 'buying traffic" (prospects that are actively looking to buy) to your website. If you are looking to raise awareness and educate, the broad keywords (in this example, "used car") will suffice. But if you are looking for someone to come to the website to purchase, then the buy keyword is the important one.

This is the first stage of the decision making process when it comes to keywords. The goal here is to understand why we are coming up with these keywords in the first place.

The second stage is that you need to use knowledge of the business to come up with the keyword. Once you do the research and come up with keywords that prospective buyers will use, you then need to dig deeper. You need to drill down further than the tool, add or modify these keywords as appropriate.

There are two schools of thoughts about keyword lists – yes, it has become a discipline on its own to have "schools of thoughts". One school of thought argues that you should target a big list of keywords. For example, they say "if you do not have a list of 1500 to 2000 keywords, then you are missing out on prospective customers searching for those keywords". The other school of thought is based on evidence – 80% of traffic comes from 20% of the keywords. Identifying those important 20% will help correctly optimize your site and will reduce the website management work.

One solution is to develop a large list of keywords – collected from tools and your knowledge of the business; then work through them to identify approximately 10 keywords that are important.

Into your prospect's mind

The final stage of determining keywords for your website is to avoid using jargon.

In the IT industry, there is a term called "disaster recovery". If you are an IT company, and you use this as your keyword, you will likely get unnecessary people coming to your website. You'll get those people who are interested in disaster recovery for floods, disasters, earthquakes and the like. What the IT company sells for 'disaster recovery' is back up and such.

Someone was selling lamps and had a keyword called 'night stand'. When he reviewed the analytics he found that many visitors were searching for 'one night stand' and arrived at his site. He then fixed it. You need to be careful about the connotations keywords too.

Another example is a cosmetic surgeon using the keyword "rhinoplasty" as their main keyword. They eventually learnt that most patients use the keyword phrase "nose job". Make sure to know how the customer refers to the search term, not necessarily how you refer to it.

When it comes to keywords, remember the 3 rules, T – B – J:

1) T – Understand the **type** of keyword your search tTerms are. Are they broad or specific?
2) B – Make sure it makes sense with your **business** model and think with the buyer in mind. Add or modify as appropriate.
3) J – Don't use **jargon**.

Be determined to understand your prospect – their frame of mind and their intentions when searching the Internet. For instance, the goal for a person searching "migraine" is different from one searching for 'migraines'. The first one may be suffering from a migraine and looking for a remedy, while the latter perhaps is doing a study.

If you ask your marketing consultant to decide on the keywords for your site, they will do it but probably with several problems. No one understands your business (and your customers) like you do. So, let them do the research but you have a final say in the keyword selection.

CHAPTER - SEVEN

NEVER LOSE ANOTHER SALE

The 80-20 Rule

I'm a big fan of the 80-20 principle. Richard Koch wrote a series of books about the concept of 80-20. As most of us know, the thought behind 80-20 is that 80% of the result comes from 20% of the effort. For instance, 80% of income comes from 20% of our customers.

Let's dissect a bit. If we have 100 customers that spend a total of $100,000 in a year, then using the 80-20 rule, $80,000 comes from our top 20 customers and the remaining $20,000 comes from 80 of our customers.

When we think in these terms, you can understand the theory's importance. It's an interesting phenomenon, because it is essentially endless. If you strip it down even further and look at those 20 customers and the $80,000 they spend, you will find that 80% of the $80,000 comes from 20% of the 20 customers. That is $64,000 that comes from 4 customers. Yes, only 4 customers. You'll often see that the top 4 to 5% of your customer base are really the ones making the strongest contributions and helping your business grow.

Where to be Careful

If we look at 80% of the people who come to your website and register, and you apply the above rule, can you assume that 20% will be buying from you, and the other 80% will go away? If we assumed that, then we would likely assume that we should forget about the 80% and just focus on the 20% who will buy.

Cirrus Decisions, a research company in the US, identified that 80% of prospects who come to a site, may not buy immediately. If you follow the 80-20 rule, you will probably disqualify that 80%. Of this group of 80%, however, Cirrus found that 70-80% of them bought the product a bit later from the competition.

Often, when you receive a lead, the lead does not show enough interest to buy. You might then classify them as "tire kickers" and disqualify them. However, what you may not know is that they are not yet ready to buy, and that they are likely to buy from you if you "help them buy".

Look at the picture below. The buying process and the selling process are not the same. When the buyer is still in the early stages of their research (for instance, they may have made an inquiry but have not properly defined their "problem"), you already may be looking to close the sale.

By disqualifying too soon, you actually lose the sales from 80% of the prospects.

The sales cycle that we use is to identify a lead, present a proposal, and convert to a customer. The purchase cycle works very differently. The customer first becomes aware of the problem, researches it, finds out about the available alternatives, evaluates their options, makes a decision, and then purchases. The two cycles – sales and purchase – don't necessarily match.

Just because someone is interested in information, doesn't mean they are going to buy. Those that aren't buying immediately should not be discounted. We need to realize what stage of the purchase cycle they are in. Be patient, so when they are ready to buy, they will.

Remember, they don't buy according to sales peoples' wishes – at least not anymore. Most purchase decisions nowadays are made by committees or a family unit. They take their time to understand the problem, the alternatives, and the solution. I've got a poster in my office that says:

They will buy when they are ready; not a moment sooner.

It's a good quote to keep reminding yourself of.

Lead Nurturing

The key in ensuring that you win the 80% of the potential sales is by nurturing the lead. You can do this by keeping them informed with relevant information. To do this, you need to identify which stage of the purchase cycle they are in and then educate and entertain them.

Keep sending this relevant information and keep doing a 'touch point' with them as they decide. This is not a sales push- it's an information feed.

Ensure what you give is valuable content and not sales oriented in any way. Distribute it in a simple and timely way through auto responder systems. These are easily available online and allow interaction in a non-intimidating fashion.

Just feeding the information via emails is not always the best option. If you don't have any interaction with the prospective customer, you may not know what they are thinking or going through. It is better for you to mix the auto responder emails with personal contacts – for instance, phone calls to see if you can help them further, or if you should disqualify them.

When it comes to nurturing leads through out a customer's purchase cycle, the largest element is to come at a situation as a problem solver offering help and advice to prospective customers.

The benefit? The opportunity is to become a trusted partner in the eyes of the customer.

CHAPTER - EIGHT

INSIGHTFUL INTELLIGENCE THROUGH ANALYTICS

You know that it is important to measure your online (and offline) marketing activities - you can't manage what you don't measure,right? However, measuring inappropriate variables will get you reports that are not useful.

Avinash Kaushik, a Google Analytics evangelist, once said that when we don't know the answers to simple questions we come up with complex reports. For example, like how the sun was positioned when the visitor was on our site! The data will be absolutely true but completely useless.

If we don't know the basics of how our marketing efforts are working, or if they are meeting our business objectives, are we really benefiting from what analytics is supposed to deliver? The analysts can give you plenty of reports – starting from what browser the visitors used, how many visitors you had on specific dates, how long they stayed on each page, where they come from – the list goes on and on. What does this mean though? You guessed it – not too much.

So what?

The analyst (whether they are working inside your organisation or as an outsourced service provider) needs your direction. You will need to share your business objectives with the analyst, so that they come up with the relevant Key Performance Indicators (KPIs).

The best way to get useful information is to start asking "so what" when the analyst provides information. For instance, your analyst reports that you got 500 visitors on Thursday and 800 visitors on Saturday, last week. Ask "so what"?. The analyst scratches his/her head and goes back to drill down. They come back and tell you these visitors were from various sources (e.g. direct traffic, advertising, Facebook etc). You ask "so what"? again. As you go, continue with your "so what?" question. They eventually tell you that of the 500 visitors on Thursday, 53% came from Facebook. And of the 800 visitors on Saturday, 72% came through Pay per click advertising campaign.

Now, you have something to dig further – why didn't you get enough traffic on Thursday from Pay per click; why was there not much traffic from Facebook on Saturday? As you analyse the data, together with your analyst, they say: "there was a lot of competition for Pay per click on weekdays, but there was very little competition on Saturday. That is, you were the only one advertising on Saturday. That is why you had more visitors and most came from Pay per click advertising campaigns." Then, you can consider what else you can do for Saturday to improve the traffic and/or conversions; what you should do to get more Facebook traffic etc.

The original information about 500 and 800 visitors was correct, but it won't give you insights to take action. When the analyst told you that 72% of the visitors came through Pay per click advertising, these aren't just numbers anymore – they are insights into your customer base. Most importantly, you can take action!

You may want to train your analyst to ask themselves, "What does that mean?" for the information they gather. They should continue to ask "what does that mean?" until they are able to translate the numbers into useful business decisions.

Metrics and KPIs

What we get when we measure the variables is called the metrics. There are plenty of metrics available. Looking through so many variables is not only useless but can also cause confusion. If you, however, define the KPIs, then the analyst can use the metrics to develop measurement against the established KPIs.

Understanding Analysis

It is important that you be as specific as possible about your KPIs.

Pat LaPointe, from MarketingNPV, demonstrated the problems of not being specific in our objectives.

He asked "Are fat people lazy?" in an article for MediaPost. He then explained that it is not easy to provide a specific answer to such a broad, non-specific question. To answer this loaded question, we would have to:

1. Define "fat."

   Weight/height ratios, body mass index, and body fat content can all be legitimate options, but a common definition would have to be agreed upon before we start the calculations.

2. Define "lazy."

   Same problem. What is lazy? Levels of exercise? Work habits?

3. Define the standard of proof.

   Just how fat is fat, and just how lazy is lazy?

4. Design a means of observing if the question is true.

   Conduct the research and collect the data.

You can see that if we don't define the terms (or the problems you are solving for) and keep the definitions "tight," politics will start entering the effort. It is, therefore, imperative that you define the KPIs tightly, and then give these to your analyst.

Get the most out of your Analyst

Before you tell the analyst what you want, take some time to truly think about what you want.

Firstly, you need to be crystal clear about your business, your goals, and the results you want to achieve. You, then, need to understand the metrics that will give you this insight. If your goals are related to branding, ensure that your metrics are too. If you're after customer service related insights (and KPIs), your analytics request should be based around this theme.

Set analytical objectives and stick to them for a while, so that you will have history to measure and compare against.

Since this is critical to your business, you should feel empowered to push the analysts to drill deeper so you can gain these insights. Make them understand the importance of this – they will start to understand that they can make a difference for you .

How to use the KPIs

When you get insights from your analytics, make sure you use them to make changes to your marketing efforts including website. Then test to see if they actually work. Measure to see the results. Whatever the experts might ask you to do, the only proof of whether it works is in implementing and measuring them. It is better to do one experiment or test than have 1000 'expert' opinions.

Once you find out what works and what doesn't, you can then change these again.

Test → Measure → Change

CHAPTER - NINE

FORGOTTEN ROAD TO CUSTOMER ACQUISITION

With the advent of emails, we are bombarded daily with a variety of emails such as newsletters (called eZines), emails about special offers, new products and services etc. From my experience in my own business, recipients of these emails get so many of them that they usually ignore most of them except the well-written email newsletters.

In the land of email SPAM, eZines tend to stand out. However, the printed newsletters stand out even more. We tested and found out that it took roughly 24 months to convert an eZine recipient for an IT services business to a customer and it took only 9 months to convert when they received the printed newsletter.

Even though this book is about online marketing, I am recommending that you do a printed newsletter rather than an eZine, simply because it works. Newsletters work regardless of the type of business, whether you are a moving company (B2C) or an IT company (B2B). It is a sneaky ("under the radar") "below the line", as the marketers would call, kind of promotion but not seen as a promotion by the recipients. There is no better fence than this. Period.

Test it and see for yourself.

Sending out boring emails work!

Don't send out newsletters every 2 or 3 months and expect to see the results. You must do the newsletters every month and send them out exactly around the same time, every month.

I found out that one of my newsletter clients (we write newsletters and mail them out on our clients' behalf) had success by sending the same (not-so-brilliant) email message to his customer list week after week. You may wonder if that is too often. Probably yes but it worked. He did get responses from his customer base that increased his sales. He said that he sent the messages weekly because he didn't know when the prospect will buy so he kept reminding them. He sent the same message because he never had time to write new message and it is better than nothing. So, make sure you are consistent and regular with your eZine or printed newsletters before expecting magical results.

Where is this road taking us?

The idea of newsletters is not new. However, with the new social media we are now focussed (and vendors recommend) on the new ways to appeal to our prospects and customers by abandoning the old ways, even when the old ones work.

Anyone who sends out newsletters consistently will tell you that they work – they create new sales. There are also online marketers that promise videos on YouTube, Tweets and blogs etc work. They probably do – but that doesn't mean you stop going on the familiar road to acquire new customers. Why do we stop doing something that works? Are we insane? If you like, use the new media in conjunction with your traditional methods of increasing sales.

How about you acquire prospects using online methods and then send them printed newsletters?

Why do newsletters work?

The main reason why newsletters, in general, work is that people don't feel like they are being sold to and the articles in the newsletters are informative and entertaining rather than selling something. Even in the advertising field, as David Ogilvy, the legendary ad man said, people are open to reading an advertorial piece that is going to assist them in some way rather than an ad.

A number of our own customers said that the printed ones work as they find reading it relaxing, entertaining and informative. It is something that they can pick up when they are doing something boring or put it in the common areas of the office for others to read when they have time.

Sometimes my clients get calls from prospects that they didn't know. They ask about a service that was written about in the newsletter – they got the newsletter from a friend to whom we sent or they have read the newsletter while waiting in someone's office. Newsletters have this "pass-along" value.

Some of our clients bind 12 or 24 months of newsletters together and send them to their prospects as part of their 'Intro package' since these newsletters are a resource.

By the way, I've read studies that say newsletters are three times more likely to be read than publications with advertising.

How can the newsletters help?

- A newsletter is a relationship building tool. You don't have to write all about your business or your technology. As their reading enjoyment increases they start looking forward to receiving your newsletter.
- A newsletter is a branding tool. If branding is to get the buyers to happily pay an irrational premium price for your product, then that is what newsletter will help you achieve. If you get your newsletter content right and the frequency of the newsletter right then your readers will love you and start building a bond with you – sometimes an invisible bond. That bond will let them buy from you without considering the competition! Am sure, you won't believe me – test it and see it for yourself.
- A newsletter is not about selling anything. My rule is 80% of the newsletter needs to be about informing and entertaining the reader. This part has to steer away from selling anything as it needs to focus on the audience and not on the company.
- Newsletters have a long shelf life. Once you have created a newsletter, you can place it on the website. You can also give out the past newsletters to sales people to distribute when they are visiting prospects or clients.
- Make it a point that in your newsletter you refer back to your website so you can drive more traffic to the sites.
- Newsletters help build your credibility. Not only do you have the opportunity, in the newsletter, to demonstrate your knowledge in your field of expertise but also show how

your other clients benefit from your expertise, through case-studies.

- Newsletters engage the readers. Every month, in one of our newsletters we give out double movie passes. In each newsletter, we have a trivia contest and the first person who calls in gets the double passes. It costs us $30-$40 and you may be surprised to know that we get CEOs from large companies phone in with the answers. The main reason they participate in this is that it is fun. Probably, like most of us, they are bored in their office and like to have a bit of fun.

List of excuses – pick your favourite!

All businesses can benefit from committing to produce a newsletter for their customer base. We know this already but most don't do it. Here are some of the common excuses:

I don't know what to write

One of our clients is a pest control company. If we write about their technology or the chemicals or the bugs, it will put the readers off. In their newsletter, we have some alerts (e.g. "winter is coming, get your office and home protected" or "new types of threats for your office") and sometimes we have case-studies. The rest of this two page newsletter has articles about general office issues, internet issues, children issues, cartoons and quotes.

You may ask what the pest control service has to do with office and the other issues. You are right, nothing! It has a lot to do with the people who read them. The newsletter is about the reader – not about the sender. Write articles that your reader will enjoy while getting educated about the need for the kind of services you offer.

Case studies are a great inclusion in any newsletter. Using this method allows you to highlight all that you do. Remember that many of your customers may only use one specific service/product so explaining how you've solved problems that fall under other categories will help your customers understand how it fits their needs. You can also discuss projects that you are working on. This is a way of communicating what you do by a sharing versus sales approach.

I do send newsletters out but we didn't see the results

If you sent the newsletters with relevant content and consistently it is almost impossible not to get results.

The most important thing you have to do in a newsletter is to make sure it goes out on time and never miss one. If you have to miss distribution of a newsletter, inform your newsletter list. However, don't miss sending them out as you will lose momentum. If you fail to keep the momentum, you risk losing all that equity you've built over the duration of the newsletter.

Make the newsletter clean, don't use too many fonts.

I am too busy to write

If you don't have anyone in your organisation to help write, then outsource the job. Like us, there are others who provide this service. In fact, when you outsource this work, everything can be done by your provider – from designing, to writing to printing and mailing, every month, without fail.

Outsourcing is expensive

I firmly believe if someone says that it is expensive to get the newsletters done regularly, then they don't know either the true cost of acquiring their customers or the life time value of their customers.

On the other hand, if you have a cash-flow issue then most likely you will have enough time on your hands. You can write the newsletter – Microsoft Office has templates for newsletters. Print them and mail them by yourself.

CHAPTER - TEN

INDUSTRY PRACTICES

What are common industry practices to drive your business forward?

Pricing

When you work with internet marketing consulting firms, you will usually find them using one of these pricing models:

a. **Keyword based pricing.**

   The provider charges the fee based on how many keywords, campaigns or ads they need to manage. Even though this is typical for Pay-per-click advertising, we have seen some firms use this model for search engine optimisation (SEO) services.

b. **Percentage of spend pricing.**

   In this model, the charge is a certain percentage of the monthly spend. This is typically used for Pay-per-click advertising – it usually ranges from 18% to 28%.

c. **A la carte**

   In this model, each and every service the provider offers is given in a services menu and you choose what is relevant. Some firms group some of these services and offer a package – e.g. Pay-per-click package, Analytics package etc.

d. **Fixed, flat fee**

   In this model, the provider charges a single fee, usually monthly, to do all the work you require related to online marketing.

Usually any fees charged by search engines or directories are paid as additional charges.

The consulting firms charge extra for copywriting, developing additional landing pages or mini-sites and testing. Most of the firms generally give access to Google Analytics or print out reports from Google Analytics as a part of the service. However, companies that charge higher fees (i.e. upwards of $3000 per month) tend to give more detailed and meaningful reports.

Contracts

Firms offer different types of contracts, including:

a. Medium to long – term: Some firms require you to sign a contract that can typically vary from 12 to 36 months.

b. Month to month: Some firms allow flexibility for customers by offering more relaxed agreements.

Managing the website

To manage the website, there are many content management systems available in the marketplace, including paid and open – source options.

I think Wordpress is one of the best content management system and platform for developing and managing websites. Since it is open source, you don't need to pay any money for this system.

Before you get started, understand your needs – how often will you be updating the site, how flexible are you with the layout and are there any special elements you need it to do. Research the different options out there to reach the optimal decision. In this day-and-age, there is something out there for almost everyone.

CHAPTER - ELEVEN

SELLING ONE AT A TIME

You want your website visitors to converted to be 'leads', right? This is where **landing pages and mini-sites** come in - to help increase your rate of conversion. If you group all the products on the website, you may not be able to give special attention to specific products. If you, on the other hand, have "landing pages" or "mini-sites" for specific products, you will be able to get better attention from your visitors.

Should you use a landing page or a mini-site? That is the question.

Landing Pages

Landing pages are web pages that are created for specific purposes. For example, if your website sells home electronics, you may have a specific page for Sony LCD TV. That is a landing page for Sony LCD TV. Usually, these pages focus on making a visitor buy or use your product or service or to at least instigate the visitor to take an action that leads to a sale.

Tips for creating landing pages

1. **Avoid distractions.** Make sure you don't create any distractions for your customers in the form of unnecessary images and links on the page, as you may end up losing them before they actually read what you have to offer and tell them.
2. **Make an offer.** Your landing page can improve your conversion rates if it presents an offer to visitors. Once

visitors receive special offers that require them to visit your landing page to learn more and take advantage of it, there is a higher chance of a conversion rate.

3. **Allow them to take action.** Make sure your landing page has an appropriate 'call to action' for the visitor to follow, that benefits you and your company.

Benefits of using landing pages to increase conversion rates

1. **Timing is everything.** With the help of the right tracking tools in the landing pages, you can find out when your visitors had responded, what they did in the landing page and if your marketing techniques were indeed worthwhile.
2. **Content management.** With content updating tools on the site, you can easily update the content on the landing page. This helps you vary your offers, update messages and also speak to different audiences.
3. **Simplicity.** When compared to a site, a landing page is much easier to set up.
4. **The seasonality factor.** Landing pages are great for use with seasonal offers as you don't have to spend too much time or money creating a page for offers that you will be using only for a few days or weeks a year.
5. **Previews.** Landing pages help you pre –sell to your prospects, which in the process, helps you increase your conversion rates.

Mini-sites

Mini-sites usually have 1-5 pages and may have a blog attached to them. Mini-sites help make money by focusing on a niche or a specific product theme.

Mini-sites work like any website but they only focus on a single topic, product and service. Today, most companies realise and agree that it's better to have various mini-sites to generate money for them than one single, large website.

Like a landing page, you have to work at successfully keeping visitors on your site by providing them with information they are looking for, and the right call to action instructions to generate conversions.

Benefits of mini-sites to increase conversion rates

1. **Self-service site.** Once you reach a fixed point, the mini-site starts generating money for you without your having to worry much about the site

   Sometimes, the techniques that you had used in the site before may not be as effective or useful to you today. So this means that you have to regularly optimize it.

2. **Focused approach.** Mini-sites help focus, making it much easier for visitors to navigate than large sites, and helps visitors easily find whatever they are looking for.
3. **Simple maintenance.** Mini– sites are easy to maintain as they have a targeted topic. It's also easier to get rid of a mini-site than to overhaul a large website if you have no need of the website in the future.
4. **Google loves them.** The search engine ranks mini-sites high, especially those with blogs as they have fresh content added to the blog regularly.
5. **Same benefits as landing pages.** Of course, don't forget that mini-sites also offer all the benefits you find associated with a landing page.

The only disadvantage of mini-sites is that they take a longer time to create, and have to be constantly updated with fresh content to improve the working of the website.

So...which helps better in conversions?

If you have a site with several products or services or specials, it may be worthwhile to create landing pages for each one of them. If you have a group of products that belong to specific group e.g. server back-up services, then it will be ideal to create a mini-site.

Made in United States
North Haven, CT
12 November 2026

22200248R00028